Hank Aaron

Lauren Spencer

the rosen publishing group's
rosen
central

To my dad, who, by keeping the radio dial tuned to the
Los Angeles Dodgers, developed in me a love for the sounds
of the crack of the bat and the roar of the crowd.
And to DJ, whose New York spirit reminds me
that it's all good when you keep your eye on the prize.

Published in 2003 by The Rosen Publishing Group, Inc.
29 East 21st Street, New York, NY 10010

Copyright © 2003 by The Rosen Publishing Group, Inc.

First Edition

Library of Congress Cataloging-in-Publication Data

Spencer, Lauren.
Hank Aaron / by Lauren Spencer.
  p. cm. — (Baseball Hall of Famers)
Summary: Profiles the man who replaced Babe Ruth as
"America's Home Run King" and also set records for RBIs
and total bases run, despite the pressures of being one of the
few black major league players in the 1950s.
Includes bibliographical references and index.
ISBN 0-8239-3600-7 (lib. bdg.)
1. Aaron, Hank, 1934—Juvenile literature. 2. Baseball
players—United States—Biography—Juvenile literature.
3. African American baseball players—Biography—Juvenile
literature. [1. Aaron, Hank, 1934– 2. Baseball players.
3. African Americans—Biography.] I. Title. II. Series.
GV865.A25 S64 2002
796.357'092—dc21

2002000277

Manufactured in the United States of America

Contents

Hank Aaron, nicknamed "Hammerin' Hank" or "The Hammer," not only broke Babe Ruth's 714 home run record, he notched up a total of 755 home runs, a record that stands unbroken. Aaron overcame racial prejudice to emerge as one of baseball's all-time greats. He also holds the record for most RBIs (2,297), total bases (6,856), and extra-base hits (1,477).

Introduction

On a rainy night in Georgia in 1974, Henry (Hank) Aaron was crowned America's home run king. He took the title away from New York Yankee legend Babe Ruth, who had held the top spot for nearly forty years. Ruth had hit 714 career home runs. When Aaron hit number 715 over the wall, he broke the long-standing record for home runs hit by one player during an entire baseball career. By the time his playing days were done, Aaron had set a new standard of 755 career home runs. It's a record that still stands untouched today.

Not everyone was thrilled to see Aaron take the crown away from Ruth. As he approached Ruth's record, Aaron endured messages of hate. Many old-time baseball fans couldn't accept that Aaron, an African American, would be the new home run king.

Ruth had been an outrageous, larger-than-life personality who played for the New York Yankees, the most successful team in baseball. Aaron, on the other hand, had worked hard to establish his place in a society divided by race. Hank Aaron had let quiet dignity and his remarkable abilities on the field speak the loudest for him. He showed the world that people should not be judged or limited by the color of their skin.

Aaron had incredible staying power. He played with the National League Braves for most of his twenty-three-year career. He moved from Milwaukee to Atlanta, where the team is based today. It was at Atlanta's Fulton County Stadium, in his twenty-first season as a major leaguer, that Aaron hit the ball that smashed Ruth's record.

Unlike most athletes, Aaron's playing improved with age. His most productive years were between ages thirty-five and forty, when he slugged 203 home runs. But Aaron was more than just a great home run hitter. He broke records in a number of categories. He still holds the number-one spot in baseball for 2,297 runs batted in. He scored 2,174 runs, putting him second to Ty

Baseball cards supply many statistics about a baseball player, but they cannot tell the personal stories that make a player memorable.

Cobb. Aaron also won three Gold Gloves for his skills as an outfielder. When he left the field for the last time in 1976, Aaron had played in 3,298 games, gone to bat 12,364 times, and had 3,771 hits, just behind Ty Cobb and Pete Rose. His numbers remain astounding, even when compared to today's sluggers like Barry Bonds and Rickey Henderson, both of whose game numbers are a few thousand shy of Aaron in running and batting. Aaron enjoyed the glory of his outstanding athletic achievements, but he also endured more than his share of pain and tragedy.

Aaron began playing baseball in the 1950s, a time of racial segregation in the United States. African Americans did not have the opportunities in sports then that they do today. Until 1947, when Jackie Robinson signed with the Brooklyn Dodgers, there were no black players on any major league baseball teams. Even after Robinson entered the majors, it was decades before professional baseball was fully integrated.

Before 1947, professional black athletes could only play baseball in the Negro leagues. These leagues had great players like pitcher Satchel Paige and outfielder James "Cool Papa" Bell, but the national media largely ignored them.

In 1920, Andrew "Rube" Foster, owner of Chicago's American Giants, joined white owners of seven teams from the Northeast and Midwest to form the Negro National League. Eight teams played a shortened summer season, which ranged from forty to sixty games.

In 1923, the Eastern Colored League was formed, opening the way for a Negro World Series between the National and Eastern Leagues.

By the mid-fifties, a few African Americans were playing on major league baseball teams. The National League seemed to be more open to change. Yet even as Hank Aaron, Willie Mays, and Ernie Banks were breaking new ground, major league baseball was still made up of less than 8 percent African Americans. Despite the low numbers, black players were among the best players of the game. Of the ten Most Valuable Players recognized by the National League in the 1950s, eight were black. But by the sixties, there was still only a slight rise in the number of African American players in the majors.

As Aaron got close to breaking Babe Ruth's record, he faced constant jeering from the stands and piles of hate mail. Standing up to the pressure and humiliation, he worked hard for his team. Through his dignity and playing skills, he helped tremendously to improve race relations. Many previously prejudiced white people began to look past the color of Aaron's skin to see him as a talented ballplayer. As his fame and fortune grew, he continued to break new ground for equal rights.

With Jackie Robinson as his hero and inspiration, Hank Aaron delivered a positive message on the playing field. He proved that color had nothing to do with ability. Once his career was established, Aaron became outspoken about racial imbalances in baseball.

The bold strides of black players during the fifties preceded the civil rights movement by only a few years. Former president Jimmy Carter said, "It was racially integrated sports teams that brought about the change that I think saved the South."

Lou Brock played baseball in the segregated South and rose to fame in the early sixties with the St. Louis Cardinals. He observed, "Baseball is the background music to America. The melting pot begins to examine itself and sees all its jewels, its treasures."

Hank Aaron is a national treasure. Through his sense of fair play and his devotion to the game, he has helped create a world for people of all colors.

Journey to Excellence

Hank Aaron was born on February 5, 1934, in a segregated section of Mobile, Alabama called Down the Bay. He was the third child in a family of eight. Aaron's parents were Herbert, a dockworker, and Estella, a homemaker.

Aaron was born a day before Babe Ruth's thirty-ninth birthday. It was Ruth's last season with the New York Yankees. Although it would take years for the names Babe Ruth and Hank Aaron to be spoken in the same sentence, Aaron knew from an early age that he wanted to play baseball.

While African Americans were proud of the talents of players like Satchel Paige, Aaron's Mobile neighbor who played in the Negro leagues, in the thirties and forties it seemed a far-fetched idea that a black man could become a major league contender. Aaron was thirteen years old

Aaron was inspired by players such as Satchel Paige *(above)*, a star pitcher for the Negro league's Kansas City Monarchs. Paige got a chance to play in the major leagues in 1948, at the age of forty-one, making him the oldest rookie ever. In 1971, Paige became the first player from the Negro leagues to be elected to the Hall of Fame.

before Jackie Robinson became the first black man signed to a contract in the major leagues with the Brooklyn Dodgers.

When Aaron was eight years old, his family moved to Toulminville, Alabama. His parents bought two parcels of land and built a six-room, windowless house. The prospect of making a living as a baseball player seemed remote, but Aaron held on to his dream. He played ball every chance he got. He didn't have the luxury of real bats and balls, so he made them out of found materials. By wrapping old nylons around golf balls, tying rags together, crumpling up tin cans, or using soda-pop tops, Aaron fashioned balls to hit with a broom handle. He threw these home-made balls over the roof of the family's house and raced around to the other side to catch them.

Aaron credits living in a small town with helping him develop his baseball skills. There were plenty of wide-open spaces to play and plenty of kids to play with in his hometown. But there were no street lights in Aaron's part of town. When it got dark, the neighborhood boys played fireball. They rolled rags into a ball, dipped it in kerosene, and set it on fire. The kids hit the flaming object until the fire went out.

Young Hank Aaron had his share of injuries during these boyhood romps. He still has a small scar from when his brother Herbert Jr. batted a tin can into his face.

As a teenager, Aaron held a few odd jobs, but whenever he got the chance he would slip away to play baseball or listen to baseball on the radio. Once, during Aaron's junior year of high school, Jackie Robinson came to Mobile to speak at the local auditorium. It was 1948, and Robinson had recently broken the major league's color barrier by being signed to the Brooklyn Dodgers. Although he faced incredible racism on and off the field, Robinson still delivered a message of hope and unity. He told the mostly black audience to keep striving for their dreams, no matter what the hardships. Aaron was so inspired by Robinson's speech that he told his father he would play major league baseball before Robinson retired.

The first time Aaron played organized baseball was with an all-black, fast-pitch softball team sponsored by the city's recreation department. He was a catcher, a pitcher, and an infielder. The team was called the Braves, which was a hint of what was yet to come. Aaron was also a good football player. As a lineman on the Central High School team, he had earned a berth on the all-city squad. But Aaron worried that he might ruin his future as a baseball player if he continued with football. He was concerned that

By the time Jackie Robinson was signed by Branch Rickey to play for the Brooklyn Dodgers in 1947, the Negro leagues were falling into financial ruin. Integration of big league baseball was a good thing for the country, but it was the end for the Negro leagues because owners were selling the contracts of their best players to the majors.

Jackie Robinson had played with the Kansas City Monarchs. Don Newcombe and outfielder Larry Doby were with the Newark Eagles. Roy Campanella played for the Baltimore Elite Giants, Minnie Minosa was with the New York Cubans, and Willie Mays played for the Birmingham Black Barons.

These players were part of the Negro leagues for only a short time before they were signed by the major leagues.

he might be seriously injured during a game. He knew, too, that if he were offered a football scholarship to college, it would be hard to turn down since his mother had set her sights on a higher education for him.

When Aaron quit the football team, his high school principal was so angry he chased him down the hall waving his cane. That event drove Aaron further away from school. During the following semester, Aaron was expelled after he skipped classes to listen to Dodgers' games on the radio.

One afternoon Aaron's father found him out of school. He told Hank that he put two quarters in his pocket every morning for lunch, while he, himself, took only one. Aaron's dad went hungry so his son would have enough to eat. Mr. Aaron knew young Hank would be able to concentrate better in school with a full stomach. What Mr. Aaron meant was that he was making sacrifices so that Hank could get an education.

Hank explained to his father that all he wanted was to play baseball. They agreed that as long as Aaron kept up with his education, he could pursue his dream of a baseball career. The next fall Hank went to a private high school. Each day, after finishing his homework, he played ball.

Beginning a Life in Baseball

In the summer of 1951, when Aaron was seventeen years old, a man named Ed Scott, who was a scout for a local semi-pro team called the Mobile Black Bears, approached Aaron. He had been watching Aaron play in a Braves' recreation league softball game. Scott asked Aaron if he would play with his team for ten dollars a game. Aaron knew his mother wouldn't approve, especially since the games were played on Sundays, the day reserved for church. Scott said he would talk to her. After Scott visited her many times, Mrs. Aaron finally agreed that Hank could join the team as a shortstop for home games only.

The Mobile Black Bears players, who were mostly older men, had mixed reactions when young Aaron joined the team. He hadn't yet reached his 180-pound weight, or his full six-foot height. He stood straight up at the plate with no crouch at all. Pitchers doubted he could hit the ball. But despite his appearance, he often hit balls clear over the outfield fence.

Aaron signed on with the Milwaukee Braves in 1952 at the age of eighteen and played in their minor leagues, winning the Rookie of the Year award. This picture was taken in 1953, the year Aaron was sent to play for the Jacksonville Tars in the South Atlantic League where he was named Most Valuable Player.

During one of the Bears' games, Bunny Downs, a scout for the Negro leagues' Indianapolis Clowns, saw Aaron. He invited Aaron to play with the Clowns. Aaron knew his parents wanted him to finish school before starting his baseball career, so he told Downs that he'd have to wait a year until he graduated. And he would need permission from his parents.

Early Integration of the Major Leagues

In 1884, Moses Fleetwood Walker and Welday Walker, African American brothers, played on a major league baseball team in Toledo, Ohio. But integration was short-lived after laws were passed banning black players from major league ball fields.

Downs told Aaron that he would wait. Aaron thought Downs would forget about him, but soon after his eighteenth birthday, an Indianapolis Clowns contract arrived. It guaranteed him $200 a month. He would need to be in Winston-Salem, North Carolina, for spring training. For Hank Aaron's family, the money was tempting, even though it meant that Hank would have to leave home before he graduated from high school. Hank promised his mom that if he made the team, he would finish high school in the off-season. If he didn't make the team full-time, then he would finish high school and enroll in college.

Some **Negro** league teams incorporated comedy routines into their on-field activity. The Indianapolis Clowns, Aaron's team, was most notable. Their antics included having players wear dresses and tuxedos. The Clowns performed and played baseball for African American fans. Their comedy brought fans into the ballpark, and their fine baseball skills kept fans coming back.

In May 1952, Hank Aaron, wearing his sister Sarah's hand-me-down pants, and carrying two homemade sandwiches from his mom, climbed into the black section of the segregated train. He traveled out of Alabama for the first time in his life. He carried a note from Ed Scott to Bunny Downs that said, "Forget everything else about this player. Just watch his bat."

Entering the Big Time

When Hank Aaron reached the Clowns' training camp in 1952, the Negro leagues were in a sharp decline. Many black fans were beginning to follow major league baseball as the major league teams slowly became integrated.

The Indianapolis Clowns had survived because they mixed cabaret and baseball. The team depended as much on their comedy routines as on their ability to play the game. There was Richard "King" Tut, who wore a tuxedo and top hat while playing along with his sidekick, a dwarf named Ralph "Spec" Bebop. Reece "Goose" Tatum, from basketball's Harlem Globetrotters, performed for the Clowns holding a three-foot-long baseball mitt. He wore a woman's dress and threw confetti at the crowd.

Although it seemed incredible that Aaron's talent could shine through all the gimmicks, he had a great first season playing shortstop. He hit well over .400. It was a hard time for him. He suffered from intense homesickness and worked very hard to be accepted by the team.

When Aaron first arrived for spring training, the other players were worried. The Indianapolis Clowns were one of the last remaining Negro league teams. They knew that if Aaron played, one team member would no longer be needed. There were very few jobs for black players in the majors. Aaron's teammates were protective of their positions. They had won the last two Negro league Eastern Division championships and were drawing crowds with their cabaret-style shows. But despite the chilly reception he first received, Aaron won over his fellow players with his outstanding hitting and fielding.

Syd Pollock, the Clowns' owner, recognizing Aaron's ability, decided to make some money from that talent. In those days, team owners of the Negro leagues often sold their players' contracts to the majors. The owner of the black team usually earned a few thousand dollars, while the player himself was guaranteed only his seasonal salary, often just a few hundred dollars.

Pollock had a good relationship with major league Boston Braves' farm director, John Mullen. Pollock let him know that there was a talented eighteen-year-old shortstop on the team who was worth coming to see. Mullen liked what he saw, and Aaron agreed to a thirty-day verbal option with the Boston Braves. This meant that Aaron would continue to play with the Clowns while the Braves decided if they wanted to make a formal offer.

On the road with the Clowns, Aaron got a taste of the country's racial climate. As the all-black team crossed the country playing exhibition games, the players were rarely welcome in hotels or restaurants. Instead, they slept and ate on the bus. Once, during a rainout in Washington, D.C., the team ate breakfast at a diner behind the stadium. Aaron heard restaurant workers smash the dishes after the players had finished eating from them. "If dogs had eaten off those plates, they'd have washed them," he remembers thinking.

During a game in Buffalo, New York, a scout for the Boston Braves, Dewey Griggs, stopped by to take a closer look at Aaron. He had a few suggestions for the young shortstop: throw harder, run faster, and stop batting cross-handed, with his left hand over his right hand. Aaron, who was a right-handed hitter, had never tried to swing his bat any other way. But during his next time at bat, he stacked his right hand on top of his left, and hit the baseball cleanly over

In 1956, these two stuffed figures were hanged in downtown Montgomery, Alabama, Aaron's home state, by unidentified people protesting racial integration. Baseball may have been in the forefront of the war against racial barriers, but as Aaron experienced, black ballplayers still faced a lot of discrimination.

the fence for a home run. From then on, Aaron kept his hands uncrossed. And so began his career as a major-league power hitter.

Suddenly, the New York Giants also began to show an interest in Aaron. Pollock knew that it was time for Aaron to decide which major league team he wanted to play for.

Both teams offered Pollock an initial $2,500 for the young player. Aaron would get $350 a month from the Braves and a spot on their minor league team in Eau Claire, Wisconsin. The Giants offered Aaron $250 dollars a month to play in their Pennsylvania minor league. Neither team offered any signing bonuses. With the Giants, Aaron would have played with the great player, Willie Mays. But Aaron decided to go with the Braves. In addition to better pay, he felt that his chance of working his way up to their major league team was more realistic. The New York Giants roster was already packed with amazing players. Something else swayed his decision. The Giants had written "Arron" on his contract. The Braves had spelled his name correctly.

After two years in the minor leagues, in 1954 Hank Aaron *(second from left)* finally made it to the major league Milwaukee Braves. He is shown here with teammates *(left to right)*, Ed Mathews, Bob Hazle, Don McMahon and Wes Covington.

Aaron boarded an airplane for the first time in his life to make the transition to minor league baseball. He was one step closer to the big time—and he was terrified. It was June 1952, and he was leaving the South to play ball in a part of the country completely foreign to him; Wisconsin was in the North.

When he arrived, he checked into the local YMCA and met his two other black teammates.

Wes Covington was an outfielder, and Julie Bowers was a catcher. Although they tried to help Aaron adjust, his sense of isolation grew daily. Two weeks after he arrived, he packed the cardboard suitcase that had been given to him by Pollock as a parting gift and called home. He was lonely and depressed. He was facing constant racism. Recently, he had thrown a ball during a double play that had smacked the player on the opposing team between the eyes, knocking him out. As they carried the man off the field on a stretcher, the crowd booed. Aaron felt supremely disliked.

After talking to his brother Herbert Jr. on the phone, he reluctantly agreed to stay with the team. Herbert told him that he would be crazy to walk away from such a great opportunity, one that might never be offered again. So Aaron stayed, focused on his game, and began to lead the league in hits. As the 1952 Braves minor league season came to an end, Aaron was named Rookie of the Year.

In his second year with the Braves, Aaron was sent to play for their affiliate, the Jacksonville Tars in the South Atlantic League (the Sally League), which was notorious for its racism. Overcoming the odds, Aaron led the league with a .362 batting average and won the Most Valuable Player Award.

Making a Difference in the Game

I n his second season with the Braves organization, Hank Aaron was sent to their Class A, minor league team in Jacksonville, Florida. The team was part of the South Atlantic League (Sally League), which consisted of eight teams spread out through Alabama, Florida, Georgia, and South Carolina. The league had been formed in 1904.

An African American had never been permitted to play on a Sally League field. In 1947, before he began his career with the Brooklyn Dodgers, Jackie Robinson had attempted to play in an exhibition game at a Sally League stadium in Jacksonville, Florida. Even though half of Jacksonville's population was African American, a Jim Crow ordinance banned interracial competition on city-owned land. When a black team arrived at the field, the gates were padlocked and the game was canceled. Facing down the Jim Crow laws would become Aaron's first victory in opening up the major leagues to African American players.

In the spring of 1953, at the age of nineteen, Aaron, and teammates Horace Garner and Puerto-Rican born Felix Mantilla, were sent to Jacksonville. They were to play for the Braves' Sally League A team, the Tars. They, along with Al Israel and Fleming Reedy, who were going to a team in Savannah, Georgia, were about to break the Sally League color barrier. Aaron recognized the awesome responsibility he held. In addition to playing better than his white teammates, he had to play with grace and dignity. Aaron knew that if he gave anyone a reason to criticize his behavior, it could be the end of his baseball career. It would also be a crushing, backward step for equality.

Aaron was permitted to play on the Sally League fields because he was part of a white team. This made a lot of white people angry. Maintaining his cool during games was not easy.

Pitchers sometimes threw the ball directly at him. When this happened, Aaron calmly dusted himself off and readied his bat for the next pitch.

In addition, people in the stands were constantly shouting racial slurs at him. Although he had suffered his share of racism growing up in Alabama, enduring daily insults was extremely painful.

Aaron loved baseball. He believed that if he played well he would advance to the major leagues. These strong feelings enabled Aaron to rise above the humiliation. The fans sitting in the blacks-only section lifted his spirits by yelling encouragement for his every move.

Who really helped Aaron get through the challenges in the Sally League was the team's manager, Ben Geraghty. Aaron has said that throughout his career, he never met a manager who cared more for his players or knew more about the game. Geraghty made sure that many of the hateful messages delivered to the team did not reach the minority players. He always visited Aaron, Garner, and Mantilla on the black side of town.

Jim Crow laws prevented blacks and whites from sharing the same schools, restaurants, or public facilities. Aaron and his black teammates weren't allowed to stay in the whites-only hotels with the other players. Instead, they stayed in the houses of black people. When the team stopped to eat as they traveled on their bus, the white players would file off quietly, leaving Aaron, Mantilla, and Garner behind until Geraghty or another teammate brought them food.

Despite these restrictions and incidents, there were great high points for Aaron. Most important, his talent was being recognized by the Braves organization. They saw that he was becoming an outstanding hitter. Geraghty was extremely proud of Aaron. He told people that Aaron's skill would make the fans forget Jackie Robinson.

By the end of the season, Aaron led the Sally League in almost every offensive category. His batting average was .362. He had batted in 125 runs and had scored 115 runs. He had 208 base hits. He had rounded 338 bases and hit 36 doubles. Aaron finished second in the league,

Police arrest Bertha Gilbert in May 1964, on a disorderly conduct charge after she tried to sit at a whites-only lunch counter in Nashville, Tennessee. Segregation was a way of life in the South, and though Hank Aaron played in the major leagues, he could not stay in the same hotels or eat at the same restaurants as his white teammates.

hitting 14 triples and 44 home runs. He was voted to the Sally League's all-star team and was named the circuit's most valuable player.

The only downside to his playing was his position on the field. At the start of the season, Aaron had been assigned to second base where he made a staggering 36 errors during the season. But his talent for swinging the bat overshadowed this statistic.

Jim Crow Laws

Jim Crow laws began in the South during the late 1800s. Thought to be named after a popular character in a minstrel show, Jim Crow statutes were enforced state by state. They were meant to separate blacks from whites. After the Civil War and Reconstruction, white people in the South became afraid of losing racial control in their cities. In 1896, a Supreme Court ruling set in motion the idea of "separate but equal." Jim Crow laws allowed white city officials to create rules to prevent black people from using many public and private spaces.

In 1915, Supreme Court victories began to break down the Jim Crow laws. But it wasn't until 1954, a year after Hank Aaron broke the color barrier in the Southern Atlantic League (Sally League), that a major blow came to Jim Crow laws. The Supreme Court decision in the case of *Brown v. Board of Education* stated that separation of schools was unconstitutional. The Civil Rights Act of 1964, the Voting Rights Act of 1965, and the Fair Housing Act of 1968 finally ended the legal hold of Jim Crow laws.

Here is a sample of Jim Crow laws instituted by Aaron's home state of Alabama:

Buses

All passenger stations in this state shall have separate waiting rooms or space and separate ticket windows for the white and colored races.

Railroads

The conductor of each passenger train is authorized and required to assign each passenger to the car ... when it is divided by a partition designated for the race to which such passenger belongs.

Restaurants

It shall be unlawful to conduct a restaurant or other place for the serving of food in the city at which white and colored people are served in the same room, unless such white and colored persons are effectually separated by a solid partition extending from the floor upward to a distance of seven feet or higher, and unless a separate entrance from the street is provided for each compartment.

Pool and Billiard Rooms

It shall be unlawful for a colored and white person to play together or in company with each other at any game of pool or billiards.

Moving Forward

At the start of his season with the Jacksonville Tars, Aaron had seen a young woman named Barbara Lucas going into the local post office. After meeting her parents, he began to date her. When the baseball season ended, Aaron proposed. From the banquet where he was accepting his Most Valuable Player award, Aaron called Barbara and asked her to marry him. She told him that he would have to ask her father. With permission from Barbara's father, the two were married a few days later in Jacksonville, Florida. Barbara and Aaron had a honeymoon of sorts when he was sent by the Braves to play for the Caguas team in Puerto Rico during the winter season.

After a miserable start to the season as second baseman, Aaron was switched to the outfield. This move kept him from being sent home to Mobile.

Aaron had accomplished a lot in his first season of Sally League play. He had broken the color barrier and had improved his baseball skills. The boos hurled from the stands had

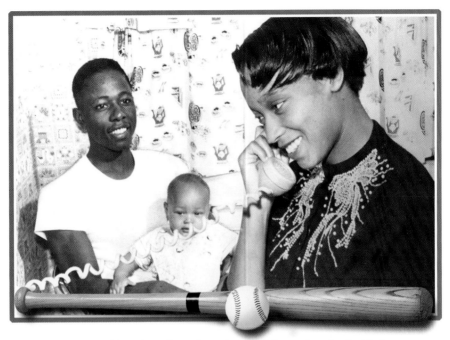

Aaron holds his son, Henry Jr., as his wife receives a call from a fan after he hit the winning home run which secured the 1957 National League pennant for the Braves and took them to the World Series against the Yankees. Aaron said in later years that this, not hitting home run number 715, was the happiest moment of his life.

subsided substantially. A columnist for the *Jacksonville Journal* wrote that he believed "Aaron may have started Jacksonville down the road to racial understanding." Hank Aaron felt that this was one of his most important achievements.

By the start of his next season with the Braves, Aaron had increased his batting average and found a new position to play on the field. And he and Barbara also celebrated the birth of their daughter, Gaile.

In 1966, the Braves moved to Atlanta, the hometown of civil rights activist Martin Luther King Jr. Deeply influenced by Dr. King, Aaron mentioned the slain leader in his speech after he hit his 714th home run. Aaron continues to speak for equal opportunity for African Americans in baseball as managers and in front-office positions.

By 1954, racial issues were gathering momentum in the United States. During that year, Ralph Abernathy and Martin Luther King Jr., two Montgomery, Alabama, ministers, began to talk seriously about delivering their message of equality to a wider audience. That year the Supreme Court had unanimously voted, in *Brown v. Board of Education*, that schools divided by race were unconstitutional.

The world was changing a little bit at a time when Aaron prepared to step before a major league audience.

In 1954, when he arrived at the Braves' Bradenton, Florida, spring training camp, Aaron felt ready for a shot at their major league team, which had moved from Boston to Milwaukee the year before. But when he looked around, he realized that the roster was already full of talented outfielders. Then, on March 13, during an exhibition game in Florida, the Braves' left fielder, Bobby Thompson, slid into second base and fractured his ankle. The next day, Aaron found himself assigned to Thompson's position on the field. During his first time at bat, he cracked the ball over the outfield fence for a home run!

As the regular season got under way, Aaron was given a Braves' uniform with the number 5 on it, a major league contract, and a place in the starting lineup, where he would remain for almost twenty-three years.

In those days, baseball teams often played what were called barnstorming games. They would join up with another team and play games

Aaron began to excel in 1957, when two changes were made: He went from second in the batting order to fourth, and he switched from a thirty-six-ounce bat to a thirty-four-ounce model. The changes paid off as Aaron led the league with 44 homers that season.

in the cities that were on their way from the Florida spring training camps to their hometown stadiums. That year, the Braves were on the road with the Brooklyn Dodgers. During the trip, the black players from both teams stayed in the same hotels. Hank Aaron spent his evenings listening to his hero Jackie Robinson, of the Dodgers, talk to teammates Don Newcombe, Roy Campanella, and Joe Black about the state of African Americans in baseball and the world. It was during these rap sessions that Aaron realized how crucial it was for him to excel at his sport and to set a good example on and off the field. He felt these hotel room meetings became his college education. Baseball was slowly working its way toward integration, but it wouldn't be until 1959, when the Boston Red Sox signed Pumpsie Green, that every major league team had a black player.

Unfortunately, Aaron's first season as a major league baseball player ended badly. With only a week left to play, he sprained his ankle. Aaron had hit only 12 home runs, and the Braves finished well out of first place.

But Aaron had gotten a taste of the excitement and wonder of major league baseball. He was thrilled to feel the support of the fans. Even though Milwaukee was the smallest city in the major leagues, people from as far away as Minneapolis would show up for games. In Aaron's first season with the team, print orders for tickets were huge. Over two million people were drawn to Milwaukee County Stadium, breaking the National League's attendance record.

Heading for the World Series

The Milwaukee Braves ended the next season a distant second to the Brooklyn Dodgers. Although 1955 was a letdown for the team, Aaron's game was improving. He was switched from left field to right. He changed his uniform number from 5 to 44, after telling the Braves that he wanted a number with two digits. That number would prove prophetic, since Hank Aaron ended up hitting 44 home runs in four different seasons during his career.

During Aaron's first season, he was given a number 5 jersey. When he later requested that it be changed to a double-digit number, he was given number 44. Uncannily enough, he went on to hit 44 home runs in four different seasons during his career.

The first season that Aaron hit more than 20 home runs was in 1955. This was a pattern he would repeat for the next twenty years. His batting average rose to .300. He scored 100 runs, and drove in 100 players. He also acquired the nickname "Hammerin' Hank."

A sportswriter who watched a homer fly off Aaron's bat and into the second-level seats at New York's Polo Grounds wrote, "Hammerin' Hank nearly tore through the balcony." Aaron was voted onto the National League's 1955 all-star team. This was the beginning of another tradition, as Aaron returned to the all-star team each year for the next twenty years. He joined Willie Mays in setting the all-time record for most all-star game appearances.

Aaron got a raise after the season ended. He would now be paid $17,000 a year to play the game he loved. While this was more money than Aaron had ever made, it pales in comparison to contracts today. In those days most players worked in the off-season to maintain a steady income. They were paid to play in exhibition games. Sometimes they got jobs outside baseball.

That year, Aaron went home to Mobile, Alabama, and became the physical fitness director for the city's recreation department. This helped him get in shape for his next season. When he turned up for spring training in 1956, he had grown into his frame. Weighing 180 pounds, he had built plenty of muscle.

But his new strength was not merely physical. He had learned to pay plenty of attention to the menu of pitches that were thrown his way. While he had always been patient at the plate, this season he waited for his perfect pitch. And when he found the one he wanted, he would swing for the fence, often sending the ball sailing over it.

His playing statistics rose dramatically during the 1956 season, as his batting average went up to .328. He became the second-youngest batting champion in National League history. He also excelled in the league with 200 base hits, 34 doubles, and 20 home runs.

That year the Brooklyn Dodgers were once again contenders for the 1956 National League pennant. Then in midseason, the Milwaukee

Braves moved into first place. Wisconsin ignited with home team spirit. There were Braves hairdos and Braves cocktails. Braves banners flew everywhere.

By the last week of the season, the Braves were only one game ahead. The Dodgers surged forward and captured the National League pennant. Although disappointed, Aaron realized that since it was his mentor Jackie Robinson's last season with the Dodgers, it was only right that Robinson should end his career as world champ.

The loss of the 1956 pennant in such a tight race seemed to light a fire under the Braves. Manager Fred Haney let the players know that when they reported for spring training the next year, he expected them to work harder than ever.

Winning It All

Spring training in 1957 was like boot camp for the Braves. They did sprints, push-ups, and sit-ups to get themselves in peak physical condition. The work paid off. When the season opened, the Braves won nine of their first ten games. It was also clear that twenty-three-year-old Aaron was

Mickey Mantle and Hank Aaron, two of baseball's greatest sluggers, pose together during the 1957 World Series which the Milwaukee Braves won. Though Mantle had two 50-homer seasons, they are dwarfed by Aaron's career figures. Aaron scored 219 more homers, 788 more RBIs, 497 more runs, and 1,356 more hits than Mantle.

becoming a very strong home run hitter. He had already slugged 12 homers over the fence by May, just a quarter of the way into the season. In late June, Aaron connected with the ball for 7 home runs in eight days. By the all-star break in July, Aaron's numbers were outstanding. His batting average had risen from the previous season to .347. His runs batted in were 73. He had scored 64 runs and hit 27 home runs.

But this was not enough to keep the Braves at number one. They found themselves two and a half games behind the St. Louis Cardinals. When the Braves two star outfielders, Bill Bruton and Felix Mantilla, got hurt colliding during a play, Aaron was moved to center field. Somehow the team found the strength to surge back into first place.

By mid August, the Braves were eight and a half games in front in the National League. Aaron had hammered his thirty-third and thirty-fourth home runs that month to help cement the lead. But as Milwaukee Braves fans knew only too well, baseball fortunes change in an instant.

Suddenly, the Braves lead dropped to only two and a half games. In the last week of the regular season, the Braves faced the St. Louis Cardinals at Milwaukee County Stadium. To clinch the National League pennant, they needed to win only one game. These were the days before major league baseball had three divisions, so the team that won the most games in their league would go on to the World Series.

On the frigid September night of the final game, bonfires were lit in the bullpens to warm the pitchers. The teams battled into the eleventh inning with the score tied 2–2. At 11:34 PM, with one out, and a man on first, Aaron came up to bat. He smacked a 400-foot home run over the center-field fence to clinch the game and the National League pennant. As he rounded the bases, all of the Braves' players ran to home plate to greet him. They hoisted Aaron up on their shoulders as the fans went wild. It was, Aaron says, "Like I'd been named the King of Wisconsin."

As the World Series got under way against the American League champs, the New York Yankees, the Braves had to muster all their talent and strength to play against a team that had set a staggering amount of records. With Hall of Fame players like slugger Mickey Mantle, catcher Yogi Berra, and pitcher Whitey Ford, the Yankees led the American League in hitting and pitching. Casey Stengel, their manager, had a great reputation. The Bronx Bombers (as they are known) had won

The Milwaukee Braves celebrate their victory over the New York Yankees in the 1957 World Series at Yankee Stadium in New York, as joyous fans rush onto the field. This was the only World Series the Braves would win while still a Milwaukee team.

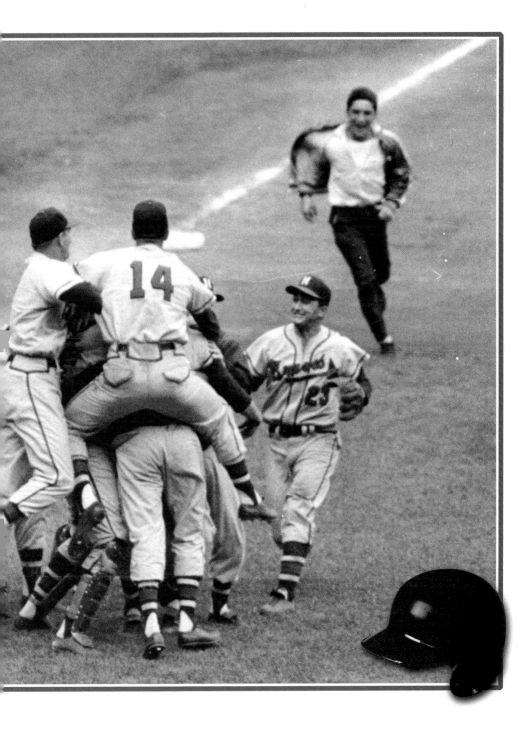

eight pennants in the last nine years. The Yankees also had held a total of seventeen world championships.

The World Series was decided by the best of seven games. The Braves would have to win four games out of seven to take home the championship rings.

The Yankees won the first and third games, and the Braves won the second. By the time the teams took the field for the fourth showdown at Milwaukee County Stadium, the players and the fans were energized. With the Braves leading 4–1 in the ninth inning, it looked like a lock. But the Yankees came from behind with a three-run homer to tie the game. It wasn't until the tenth inning that the Braves pulled ahead for a 7–5 victory, tying the series at two games apiece.

The Braves won the fifth game, forcing the series back to Yankee Stadium. Although Aaron hit his third homer of the season, the Yankees won Game 6. During the seventh and final game at Yankee Stadium, the Milwaukee Braves pulled in front early and shut out the Yankees, 5–0.

Aaron takes advantage of a bad throw by Yankee pitcher Art Ditmar to advance to second base during a World Series game in 1958. The 1958 series was almost a replay of the 1957 World Series, but this time, the Yankees came out on top.

The Milwaukee Braves had won their first World Series and Hank Aaron, with an average of .393, was voted Most Valuable Player in the National League! Aaron was now in the company of other baseball greats like Roy Campanella, Willie Mays, Don Newcombe, and Jackie Robinson. This was, Aaron says, his most satisfying baseball season ever: "It doesn't get any better than Milwaukee in 1957."

Becoming a Contender

By 1958, Hank Aaron's family had grown. A son, Henry Jr., was born in 1957. Twins, Gary and Lary, were born the following winter. Sadly, Gary died in the hospital shortly after birth.

By the start of the 1958 season, Aaron was one of the highest-paid players on the Braves and he was flying high from the previous season's successes. But he was still dealing with the challenge of being a black player in major league baseball.

It had been over ten years since Jackie Robinson had broken the color barrier, but racial segregation was still a major issue. During spring training in Florida, Aaron had never been allowed to stay at the Manatee River Hotel with his white teammates. He and the other nonwhite players stayed above the garage at the house of an African American schoolteacher and her husband. When Aaron achieved National League batting-champion status, he was allowed to move into the couple's main house.

Aaron had experienced racial prejudice throughout his baseball career. He had usually dealt with it quietly and forcefully, letting his bat do the talking. But it was becoming extremely difficult for him to hold back his feelings, especially since he had proved himself on the baseball field.

He and his teammate Felix Mantilla endured a particularly frightening event while they headed for spring training in 1958. As the two World Series champs drove down the highway in Aaron's new Chevrolet Malibu, a carload of white teenagers pulled up behind them. The teenagers tapped the bumper of the car. Intending to let the car go around them, Aaron pulled over. Instead, the car slowed down and waited for Aaron and his passenger to get back in the lane. Aaron gunned the Chevy to pass the teenagers. Next, the car of teens passed them at sixty miles an hour. They slammed the front of Aaron's car, pushing it into a ditch, from where it spun back into traffic. Miraculously, neither Aaron nor Mantilla was physically hurt. This incident caused Aaron to rethink his approach to dealing with racism. He realized that he would have to speak out in a different way. He must make himself heard beyond the crack of his bat.

Once the 1958 season officially got under way, things seemed much like the year before. The Milwaukee Braves once again captured the National League pennant. But the 1957 pennant race had been filled with a special kind of magic. The 1958 pennant win didn't seem to spark the fans or players with the same enthusiasm.

The Braves faced the New York Yankees again in the World Series. Each of the seven games was tightly scored; each was decided by one run. The Braves lost the last three games. There was no repeat of the previous year's championship parade.

But Aaron, who had played very well, won his first Gold Glove Award. He finished third in the voting for Most Valuable Player, just behind Willie Mays and Ernie Banks.

Aaron won many awards, including three Gold Gloves and two Silver Bats. He is pictured here with the Mel Ott Memorial Award, which he won after hitting 44 home runs in the 1963 season.

By the start of the 1959 season, Hank Aaron was in a groove. He was so hooked into the hitting cycle that for a while he stopped going to the movies. He didn't want anything to affect his eyes.

At first it seemed like the Braves were headed toward winning another National League pennant. But Aaron's hitting strength was not enough to hold his team in first place. By September, the Braves were already trailing by four games.

Then they surged ahead again and found themselves in a first-place tie with the Los Angeles Dodgers. The pennant would be decided by a best-of-three-game play-off.

The Braves started the series at home, but the stadium was only half full. It seemed that Milwaukee fans had been spoiled into expecting a World Series and were saving themselves for that. That expectation did not come to pass. The Dodgers won the first game and went on to win the next two games at home in Los Angeles. Winning the pennant, the Dodgers advanced to the World Series.

Making the Hits Happen

As the 1959 season ended, Hank Aaron was invited to appear on a TV show called *Home Run Derby*, which pitted two players against each other. The player who hit the most homers won. Aaron, who had never thought of himself as a home run hitter, didn't expect to do well. But he slugged the most home runs and won $30,000. That was almost two years' salary for Aaron!

Aaron realized hitting home runs was a worthwhile goal. He wryly noted, "I noticed that they never had a show called *Single Derby*."

As he steadily built up hitting power, Aaron's salary approached that of an all-star player. But the Milwaukee Braves were falling on hard times. Despite Aaron's 34 home runs and 120 runs batted in, the Braves finished the 1961 season in fourth place.

The next year, with his brother Tommie joining the team, Aaron raised his home run numbers to 40 and drove in 126 runs. The next season, he had 44 home runs and 130 runs batted in. Still, the Braves could not make the play-offs.

As the team's performance level dropped, so did attendance. The ball club struggled to survive, and rumors began to circulate that the team would move to Atlanta. The governor of Georgia had built a new stadium, hoping to attract a major league team.

By the end of the 1965 season, the Milwaukee Braves had become the Atlanta Braves. Aaron said good-bye to Milwaukee County Stadium with his 398th career home run.

S ome of the letters Hank Aaron received during his quest to break Babe Ruth's all-time career home run record were filled with hate. Some were filled with hope.

Dear Henry:

First I would like to say you are regarded by many as a good baseball player and a good hitter. To even remotely suggest that you are a great player or hitter, a person would have to be judged insane.

Dear Hank Aaron,

I hate you!!!! Your [sic] such a little creap! [sic] I hate you and your family. I'D LIKE TO KILL YOU!!! BANG BANG YOUR [sic] DEAD. P.S. It mite [sic] happen.

Dear Mr. Aaron,

For years sports fans have been waiting for the right man to come along and break that record. You, Henry Aaron are that man. You are the MESSIAH that has finally arrived.

Dear Mr. Aaron,

I am twelve years old, and I wanted to tell you that I have read many articles about the prejudice against you. I really think it's bad. I don't care what color you are. You could be green and it wouldn't matter. These nuts that keep comparing you in every way to Ruth are dumb. Maybe he's better. Maybe you are. How can you compare two people thirty or forty years apart? You can't really. So many things are different. It's just some people can't stand to see someone a bit different from them ruin something someone else more like them set. I've never read where you said you're better than Ruth. That's because you never said it! What do those fans want you to do? Just quit hitting?

Atlanta welcomed the Braves with fanfare. Aaron and his black teammates would be the first African Americans to play on a major league baseball field in Georgia. Aaron knew as soon as he walked into Atlanta's Fulton County Stadium that his home run career would take an exciting upswing. The city was at a high altitude, and the climate was hot. Both factors would help the ball carry better than it had in Milwaukee. Aaron had hit more home runs on the road than he had at Milwaukee's stadium.

During the last month of 1973 and into 1974—until he hit home runs number 714 and number 715—the umpires gave pitchers special balls with infrared code numbers on them to pitch to Hank Aaron so they could be collected and identified as souvenirs.

In 1966, during the Braves' first season in Atlanta, thirty-two-year-old Aaron became only the eleventh player in baseball history to hit 400 career home runs. Coincidentally, Babe Ruth had also been thirty-two when he reached 400 career homers. Aaron's career was beginning to follow Ruth's closely. Despite his achievement, Aaron had a tough season. Hecklers in the stands were yelling the kinds of racist slurs that he hadn't heard since his days in the Sally League.

Nevertheless, Aaron's profile continued to grow with the increase of his home run numbers. He signed his highest contract ever, $100,000 a season, putting him in the company of only five other major league ballplayers: Sandy Koufax, Don Drysdale, Mickey Mantle, Willie Mays, and Frank Robinson.

Atlanta Braves president John McHale helps Aaron try on his new Atlanta uniform after Aaron signed a new contract in 1966 worth $100,000 making Aaron one of the six highest-paid baseball players at the time.

Life at home was not happy, though. Hank and Barbara had grown apart. Divorce was imminent. Putting his energies into baseball, he began to think seriously about breaking Babe Ruth's career home run record of 714.

Adding to his heartache, there had been a fire at his home. Many of the trophies he had won during his baseball years had been destroyed.

Considering himself an all-star home run contender was helpful to Aaron. It enabled him to focus on a goal.

Approaching the Record

In the spring of 1968, Martin Luther King Jr. was assassinated in Memphis. His funeral was held in King's hometown of Atlanta the day before the first game of the Braves' season opener. There was talk of rescheduling. But Dr. King's father told the team that his son would have wanted the game to go on. Aaron felt especially committed to achieving his hitting goals while playing for the city where Martin Luther King Jr. was born.

In the middle of the 1968 season, Aaron belted his 500th home run during a game against the Giants. Aaron was thirty-five years old but still in excellent shape. In July, just ten days after U.S. astronauts became the first humans to land on the moon, Aaron hit his 537th home run. This moved him into third place on the all-time home run list. Though ahead of Mickey Mantle, he was still behind Willie Mays and Babe Ruth.

Aaron wanted to reach 3,000 career hits. At the start of the 1969 season, he was only 208 hits away. That year, the Braves made it into play-offs. They won the National League's newly formed Western Division title. They would face Eastern Division winners, the New York Mets.

After an accident at his home, Aaron played in the postseason with stitches in his hand. He was still able to hit a home run in each of the three games. Although the Mets dominated the series, winning the 1969 National League pennant, postseason play brought Aaron into an even higher profile with both the media and the fans.

In 1970, Aaron became the first black player to reach 3,000 hits. Unfortunately, his hits couldn't help the Braves. They dropped in the standings and stayed there all season.

Hank Aaron watches the ball fly after he hits his 500th home run. The three-run homer came in a 1968 game, off San Francisco Giants pitcher Mike McCormick.

In February 1971, the Aarons' divorce became final, and the slugger put all his energy into baseball. Aaron had been playing for well over a decade with the Braves when he was moved from the outfield to first base in order to rest his knee, which he had injured the previous year as he slid into home plate. But he was hitting balls out of the park faster than ever. Aaron ended the season with 47 home runs, his highest season total.

Before the 1972 season, Aaron signed a two-year contract which guaranteed him $200,000 a year. He was the first player to receive that much money. The same season he also hit his 648th home run, pulling even with Willie Mays. Aaron and Mays now shared the number-two spot for all-time career home runs.

The hits kept on coming. When Hank Aaron blasted number 660 over the fence, he broke Babe Ruth's record for most home runs hit by a player with one team. By then, the contest to beat Ruth's career home run record was big news. In addition to Aaron, the media and fans were paying rapt attention.

The Braves gave Aaron a secretary to handle the mail that poured in. Not all of it was supportive. For some people, race was still a big issue. Babe Ruth's record was sacred to them.

The Yankees' Babe Ruth had been one of baseball's most charismatic players. He was remembered as much for his antics off the field as for his ability to wallop baseballs over the fence. And he had slugged the ball again and again, until he reached 714 homers. It was a towering achievement and some fans believed Ruth's record would stand forever.

Aaron's approach to the game of baseball and to home runs was unique. Taking his stance at the plate with a quiet focus, once Aaron hit the ball, he rarely stopped to watch it leave the ballpark. On the other hand, Ruth, a.k.a. the Sultan of Swing, wore a big smile as he watched his hits leave the park. Then he would begin his clumsy trot around the bases. But in the end, what plagued Aaron the most was not the difference in their playing styles. It was the difference in their skin colors. Sadly, the home run competition gave him as much pain as it gave him joy. While he endured hecklers and threatening mail, the whole country benefited from his achievements.

The Big Game

By 1973, Hank Aaron was only 41 home runs short of tying Babe Ruth's record. Aaron had to focus on blocking out the hate-filled messages that were being sent to the Braves' organization.

Aaron decided to turn these messages into a bonus. "As the hate mail piled up, I became more and more intent on breaking the record and shoving it in the ugly faces of those bigots. I'm sure it made me a better hitter," he has recalled.

At the start of the season, the Federal Bureau of Investigation (FBI) was brought in to look over all the mail that Aaron received. They also screened the threatening phone calls being placed to his parents and his children. An Atlanta policeman named Calvin Wardlaw escorted him to and from the stadium. When a plot to kidnap his oldest daughter, Gaile, who was at Fisk University, was uncovered, several FBI agents were sent to protect her.

Aaron waits in the Braves dugout before a game in 1972. By this time, many people, including Aaron himself, thought it was only a matter of time before he would beat Babe Ruth's record of 714 home runs.

At one point, Aaron's secretary was receiving over 3,000 letters a day. Though not all of it was hate mail, there were plenty of nasty letters. Aaron warned his teammates to keep their distance in the dugout, just in case a crazed person tried to hurt him.

By the end of 1973, the U.S. Postal Service estimated that Aaron had received 930,000 pieces of mail, the most for any nonpolitician in history. Once the press began to write stories about the hate mail, Aaron began to receive more letters of support. Atlanta fans who had long been absent from the stadium began to attend games again.

Aaron, who had been receiving standing ovations in ballparks other than his own, wondered why Braves fans were being so quiet. But as the race for the home run record began to tighten, and as Aaron soldiered on, he began to hear supportive voices from his home stands.

By the all-star break of 1973, Aaron had hit his 700th homer. At the end of the season, he was only one homer short of tying the Babe's record. At his last game of the season, Atlanta's Fulton County Stadium was full. Aaron played the game without hitting one home run. For his last at bat, he hit a pop-up for an out. But it didn't matter. The fans stood and roared. It was his first ovation in Atlanta. He had not yet captured the record, but he had finally captured their hearts!

During the off-season, Aaron married Billye Williams, an Atlanta talk-show host whom he had met in 1972. While they honeymooned in Jamaica, the next season's challenge was never far from his mind.

Energy was high at the start of the 1974 season. The Braves' owners had wanted to keep Aaron out of the first three games of the season. They wanted him to tie and break Ruth's record on the home field.

But the commissioner of baseball made sure that Aaron played in the season's opening game on April 4, 1974. It was the sixth anniversary of the assassination of Martin Luther King Jr.

Batting in the top of the first inning, Aaron faced Cincinnati Reds' pitcher Jack Billingham. Aaron stood at home plate with a count of three balls and one strike. The next pitch was a sinker. He swung, sending it into the left-center-field seats. It was home run number 714. Aaron had tied Ruth's record once and for all!

"It was like I had landed on the moon," he has remembered. "All I had to do now was take the next step." After the game, Aaron held a news conference and paid tribute to Dr. King. Then he celebrated the glory of the moment with his teammates and family.

This 1973 picture shows Aaron with his soon-to-be second wife, Billye Williams, outside an Atlanta hotel where he announced that he was signing on with a management agency to handle his public appearances and commercial endorsements. By this time Aaron had hit 712 home runs. He was only two away from tying Babe Ruth's record.

This picture shows "Hammerin' Hank" Aaron, after swinging his bat in Atlanta in March 1974, one month before he finally hit his 715th home run.

On April 8, the Braves faced the Los Angeles Dodgers at home in Atlanta. It was Hank Aaron Night, and almost 54,000 people were in the stands. Pearl Bailey sang "The Star Spangled Banner." Entertainer Sammy Davis Jr. and Jimmy Carter, then governor of Georgia, were there. Aaron's father threw the first ball. The commissioner of baseball, Bowie Kuhn, did not come, sending Monte Irvin in his place. Although Kuhn's absence sent an unpleasant message to Aaron, still, he kept focused.

Aaron faced Dodger pitcher Al Downing in the bottom of the fourth inning. There were two outs and a runner on first base. The count stood at three balls and one strike. When Aaron connected with a slider that was low and down the middle, the ball soared through the air and cleared the fence.

This time Aaron actually watched his 715th tie-breaking homer fly into the stands. As he made his way around the bases, there were tears in his eyes. Aaron was congratulated by each Dodger whom he passed as he circled the field. At second base, two white college kids joined him. They had jumped on to the field from the stands to share the thrill of the moment by running with him to home plate.

Once Aaron had made it around the bases, the floodgates opened. His mother leapt onto the field and grabbed him in a bear hug, which was meant to protect him from harm as much as to congratulate him. Someone brought a microphone to home plate and stopped the game just long enough for Aaron to say, "Thank God, it's over."

Aaron eyes the ball after hitting his 715th home run, a 400-foot homer against Los Angeles Dodgers pitcher Al Downing. A crowd of 53,775 gave Aaron a ten-minute standing ovation while fireworks went off over the center-field roof.

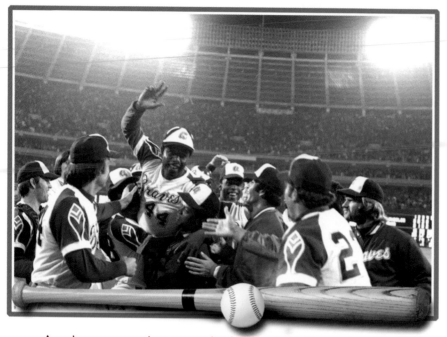

Aaron's teammates rush to congratulate him after he hit his record-breaking 715th career home run. Hank Aaron never hit 50 homers in a season, but he hit 20 or more home runs for twenty consecutive seasons. From 1955–1974, Aaron had eight seasons with 40 or more homers, including a career-high 47 in 1971. He had 63 multi-homer games, and his 16 grand slams are the most by a National League player.

Then the rain started. Since the game was only in the fourth inning, Aaron's record would have been wiped out had the bad weather continued. But the rain stopped, and the game resumed.

At the age of forty, Aaron had set a new record for all-time career home runs. As the game went on, teammate Ralph Garr spurred Aaron on to continue hitting and "break Hank

Hammerin' Hank's mother, Estella, gives him a huge hug after he broke Babe Ruth's home run record. On the right, Tom House, the Braves' relief pitcher clutches the prized ball, which he caught in the bull pen. Aaron said later that he was glad that House caught the ball and not someone who would later sell it. Both the bat and the ball from that day are kept in Turner Field (formerly Fulton Field) in Atlanta.

Aaron's record." Eventually, Aaron did break his own record. But he didn't do it during that already eventful game.

During the sixth inning, Aaron spoke with President Richard Nixon on the phone from the team dugout. When the game was over, Aaron had a party and press conference in the clubhouse. Then, he said, he went home, got down on his knees, and thanked God.

An all-star baseball luncheon was held in Aaron's honor after he broke Babe Ruth's record. He was presented with this trophy, commemorating "Baseball's Most Memorable Moment." The road that the Atlanta Braves' Turner Field is on has been named after Aaron, too.

Aaron said later that it was not so much joy as it was relief that he felt after he hit his 715th home run. He had been able to prove himself to all the people who had written him nasty letters (which he still keeps).

Aaron had said he remained a bitter man for the next few years, in spite of having broken the record. It was only decades later, as he saw integration take effect and discrimination end, that he was able to savor his victory.

New Challenges

Having become America's home run king, Aaron was now ready to begin another chapter in his professional life. Two days after his monumental achievement at Atlanta's Fulton County Stadium, the stands were less than half full, and Aaron's suspicions about the disinterest of the home-team fans was confirmed. A position managing the team had opened up, and although Aaron had been verbal about bringing more African Americans into management roles, he was conflicted about putting himself up for the job. He didn't feel ready to retire from the playing field, even though he wasn't entirely happy with the Braves.

Aaron stayed on. But as the season progressed, it became increasingly clear that 1974 would be his final year with the Atlanta Braves. He wasn't happy with the turnout at the stadium for games, and he was even less pleased with decisions being made by the people in the front office. The Braves management knew how Aaron felt and held a Hank Aaron Night in July. Throughout the season, other cities also put together festivities to mark Aaron's great achievements.

The event he remembers most vividly was held in New York City. He was invited to meet local dignitaries, as well as the wives of Babe Ruth and Lou Gehrig. He rode through Harlem and spoke to a crowd of about 5,000 people. When he looked out at the faces, he was reminded of his boyhood when he had been so inspired by Jackie Robinson's speech in Mobile, Alabama. Aaron hoped that he had delivered the same follow-your-dreams message to the crowd in Harlem.

As the 1974 season drew to a close, the Braves discussed a front-office job with Aaron. But he wanted to keep his playing options open.

His on-field averages had dropped substantially, and Aaron acknowledged that having spent his entire baseball career with an eye on breaking records, his motivation had shifted. Although he batted only 340 times during that season, he finished with a .268 average and 20 home runs. He hit only one homer during his last game for the team at Atlanta's Fulton County Stadium. Attendance had fallen down to 11,000 people.

In the off-season, Aaron traveled, finding himself in Tokyo for a home-run-hitting contest against Japanese home run champ Sadaharu Oh. The fan response there was overwhelming. He faced 2,000 reporters at the airport and 50,000 fans in the stands.

After beating his Japanese counterpart 10 home runs to 9, Aaron was awakened later that night by his friend, Milwaukee Brewers owner Bud Selig. Aaron had been traded to the Brewers. Aaron would be playing in his old stomping ground of Milwaukee. Del Crandall, a former Braves' teammate, would be his new manager.

This picture shows Aaron hitting his 754th home run in a game against the Texas Rangers in Milwaukee. Hank Aaron hit his 755 home runs off 310 different pitchers, including 12 Hall of Famers. Don Drysdale was the pitcher Aaron victimized the most. He hit the most homers against the Cincinnati Reds.

Despite switching leagues and facing new pitchers, Aaron was thrilled. He had been signed onto the American League Milwaukee Brewers as the designated hitter, a position created in 1973. The designated hitter's job was primarily to bat in place of pitchers.

Baseball fans were overjoyed by Aaron's return to Milwaukee. On a cold, 1975 opening night, 48,160 people serenaded Aaron from the stands with the words "Welcome home, Henry. It's so nice to have you back where you belong!" They sang it to the tune of "Hello, Dolly."

Aaron became a mentor to the Brewers' younger players, who often gathered around him for hitting advice. Although he was voted onto the all-star team, it seemed a sentimental move, since his numbers were severely diminishing. By season's end, he had a .234 average and had hit 12 home runs.

The possibility of becoming the Brewers' manager became real when the Brewers fired theirs. But Aaron still did not think that it was the right time. He had been heartened that the color barrier in baseball management had finally been broken when Frank Robinson was named manager of the Cleveland Indians. But he knew that there was further to go in the quest for racial equality within major league baseball.

The following year would be Hank Aaron's last on the field. He decided to retire after the 1976 season. His last home run came on July 20, against the California Angels. It was number 755. It's an all-time career home run record that

> **H**ank Aaron holds the record for hitting 755 career home runs at this writing. Babe Ruth and Willie Mays now make up the number two and number three spots, with 714 and 660 career home runs respectively.

stands to this day. He hit that final home run during his twenty-third year as a professional ball player. He was playing his 3,298th game. When he stepped up to bat, it was for the 12,364th time. At the moment of his retirement, Aaron held more records for running, batting, and playing than any man in baseball history.

A New Job

In 1976, media mogul Ted Turner purchased the Atlanta Braves. As soon as he took over the team, Turner contacted Aaron to make him a solid offer. At age forty-two, Aaron accepted a front-office job with the Braves as player development director. Since the majority of his family still lived in the South, the move back to Atlanta made sense. Now that he was off the road, he would be able to see his children more often.

Hank Aaron became responsible for the Braves' farm team system. It was a perfect place for him, since he'd come up through the organization more than twenty years earlier. He hired his younger brother Tommie to manage the Braves top farm team in Richmond, Virginia. He needed people he could trust to report back to him about player development.

It was a rare event when Aaron was able to sit in the minor league stands without being distracted by fans or reporters. By the time Aaron was promoted to Braves' senior vice president and assistant to the president in 1990, he had helped develop a team that produced National League Rookie of the Year David Justice, two-time Most Valuable Player Dale Murphy, and pitcher Tom Glavine.

The Braves continue to be one of the best teams in baseball because of the groundwork Aaron laid. At this writing, Aaron is a senior vice president and a member of the board of directors for the Atlanta Braves and the Turner Broadcasting System (TBS). He is also corporate vice president of community relations for TBS.

In addition, Aaron is involved in charity organizations that focus mostly on children. Before the end of his playing days, with the help of Brewers' manager Bud Selig, he set up the Hank Aaron Scholarship Fund to raise money to send underprivileged students to college. This organization was expanded in 1995, with the help of Turner and Aaron's wife Billye. Renamed the Chasing the Dream Foundation, it was inspired by a TBS documentary of the same name, which focused on Aaron's life as a home run hitter and civil rights pioneer. The television special won a Peabody Award and was nominated for an Oscar.

Through the Chasing the Dream Foundation, forty-four (Hank Aaron's number) kids each year are awarded financial assistance to pursue their dreams in areas ranging from the arts to sports. This support enables kids to afford instruments, lessons, equipment, and more. Aaron hopes to expand the number of children who receive help from the foundation to 755 a year, in honor of the number of home runs he hit.

In 1991, Aaron wrote a best-selling book called *I Had a Hammer: The Hank Aaron Story*. He has teamed up with Japanese home run hitter Sadaharu Oh to develop baseball in third-world countries. He has served on the executive boards for PUSH (People United to Serve Humanity) and the National Association for the Advancement of Colored People (NAACP).

Aaron also works on a variety of committees for cancer and leukemia research. His brother Tommie died from leukemia in 1984.

The Hall of Fame

In August 1982, Hank Aaron was honored for his impact on the game of baseball when he was inducted into the Baseball Hall of Fame.

In his first year of eligibility, Aaron's baseball peers elected him with an overwhelming majority. The votes came in just nine short of unanimous at 97.8 percent. The legendary Ty Cobb, with 98.2 percent of the vote in 1936, was the only other player to get a higher percentage.

Baseball commissioner Bowie Kuhn presents Hank Aaron with a plaque commemorating Aaron's 1982 induction into the Baseball Hall of Fame. Today Aaron is the senior vice president of the Atlanta Braves and assistant to Stan Kasten, the Braves' president.

Aaron found himself in good company at the induction ceremony. He was being honored along with Frank Robinson, who had been a part of Aaron's close-knit black all-stars in the fifties and sixties. Robinson was the first African American manager in the history of major league baseball. Also being honored was Happy Chandler, the commissioner of baseball who had gone against fifteen of the sixteen major league owners in order to put Jackie Robinson on the Dodgers in the 1940s.

Bowie Kuhn was at the ceremony. Although Aaron had made peace with the commissioner of baseball, he continued to have a hard time accepting Kuhn's absence at his historic home run, tie-breaking game in 1974. Aaron delivered the shortest speech of the night. He told the crowd, "It has been for me, to quote a very popular song, 'the long and winding road.'" He added that he was there because players like Jackie Robinson and Roy Campanella paved the way by proving to the world that a man's ability is limited only by his lack of opportunity.

Being honored by the baseball community in such a powerful way helped Aaron feel that he had finally been accepted by major league baseball. His journey had been one step ahead of the quest for equality in America. Today the baseball field has leveled out enough to welcome people of all colors and creeds.

Baseball Today

Aaron's ability to play great baseball year after year, and to earn the title "Home Run King" came from his mental and physical endurance. He was able to put aside racial intimidation and go forward, playing with grace and talent well into his forties.

Watching Sammy Sosa and Mark McGwire's home run race in 1998, Aaron commented that he was glad that they looked like they were having fun. This fun was something he missed while trying to overtake Babe Ruth's record. To Aaron, it seemed the fans during the Sosa-McGwire contest were not focused on the color of the face, but rather on the excitement of the chase. Barry Bonds, who broke the single-season home run record in 2001, may be a contender for Aaron's career record. Bonds, whose godfather is Willie Mays, has also broken Babe Ruth's all-time walk record of 170.

Overcoming great odds, Aaron had played baseball with heartfelt passion and love for the game. And he had tread new ground.

No multimillion-dollar contracts or valuable endorsement deals were offered to him. In fact, during his entire career, Hank Aaron endorsed just one company, Magnavox Electronics, which signed him up for $1 million over five years.

In 1999, marking the twenty-fifth anniversary of his history-making home run, Aaron was honored on Capitol Hill. He was celebrated for his great baseball achievements and named to Major League Baseball's All-Century team. Also created that year was the Hank Aaron Award, which is awarded every season in each league to the best all-around hitter. In 2000, Aaron was made a part of the fifteen-member Baseball Hall of Fame Committee, replacing Pee Wee Reece.

Hank Aaron and his wife Billye, emerge from Capitol Hill with Representatives Johnny Isakson *(left)* and Sanford Bishop *(second from left)* after Congress held a ceremony to honor Aaron on the twenty-fifth anniversary of his 715th home run.

Reflecting the dignity that has made him such a great man, Aaron acknowledges the inspiration he received from the people who came before him. In a book released for the twenty-fifth anniversary of his home run record, Aaron wrote, "I am in awe of the great home-run hitters, the ones who are no longer with us. The Reverend Dr. Martin Luther King, for one. Jackie Robinson, for another . . . Forget about Hank Aaron. King and Robinson, they're the real home-run hitters."

But history reflects that Hank Aaron's achievements both on and off the field have been instrumental in weaving a much richer American tapestry.

HANK AARON *TIMELINE*

⚾	**Feb. 5 1934**	Henry Louis Aaron is born in Mobile, Alabama, to Estella and Herbert Aaron.
⚾	**1947**	Aaron is thirteen when Jackie Robinson plays his first game on April 15 for the Brooklyn Dodgers.
⚾	**1950**	Aaron signs for $10 a game to play shortstop for the Mobile Black Bears.
⚾	**1952**	Aaron plays his first game for the Negro league Indianapolis Clowns.
⚾	**1952**	Aaron plays for the Braves minor league team in Eau Claire, Wisconsin. He is named Rookie of the Year.
⚾	**1953**	Hank Aaron, Horace Garner, and Felix Mantilla become the first black players to integrate the Sally League.
⚾	**1953**	Aaron marries Barbara Lucas of Jacksonville, Florida. They spend their honeymoon in Puerto Rico where Aaron plays outfield in the winter league for the Caguas team.
⚾	**1953**	Aaron becomes the regular left fielder for the Milwaukee Braves.
⚾	**Apr. 23 1954**	Aaron hits his first major league home run.
⚾	**1956**	Aaron wins his first National League batting title with a .326 average.
⚾	**1957**	Aaron hits his 100th home run.

⚾	**1957**	The Braves win the World Series. Aaron is named Most Valuable Player for the season.
⚾	**1959**	During the postseason, Aaron is a contestant on a television show called *Home Run Derby*. He wins $30,000, more than any other competitor.
⚾	**1962**	Aaron earns $50,000 a year. His brother Tommie joins the Braves and becomes his roommate.
⚾	**1966**	The Braves move to Atlanta.
⚾	**1966**	Aaron wins his fourth National League home run title.
⚾	**July 4 1966**	Aaron hits his 500th home run.
⚾	**Apr. 8 1974**	Aaron hits his 715th home run, breaking Babe Ruth's record.
⚾	**1974**	In November, Aaron is traded to the Milwaukee Brewers.
⚾	**Aug. 1 1982**	On August 1, Aaron is inducted into the Baseball Hall of Fame.
⚾	**1984**	In August, Aaron's brother Tommie, age forty-five, dies of leukemia.
⚾	**1987**	The Atlanta Braves become the first team in baseball with a fair-share agreement, a contract stipulating that the organization will grant minorities a fair share of everything, from executive positions to professional services. The NAACP pushed for this agreement.

Glossary

all-star game A game played between the two all-star teams in the middle of the baseball season.

all-star team A team made up of players chosen by baseball fans and the players' peers; there is one National League team and one American League team.

American League One of the two major professional U.S. baseball leagues, established in 1900. The American and the National Leagues are made up of three divisions: East, Central, and West.

barnstorming games Games played by teams on their way home from spring training; teams stopped to play in towns along the way.

base hit A hit that results in the batter safely reaching first base.

batting average   An average determined by dividing the number of base hits by the number of official times at bat. The result is carried to three decimal places. A player with 100 base hits in 300 times at bat has a batting average of .333.

Brown v. Board of Education   A decision reached on May 17, 1954, in which the Supreme Court unanimously declared that separate educational facilities are "inherently unequal" and, as such, violate the Fourteenth Amendment to the U.S. Constitution, which guarantees all citizens "equal protection of the laws."

Civil Rights Act   An act passed in 1964 by the Supreme Court that protected the constitutional rights of all people in public facilities and public education, and prohibited discrimination in federally assisted programs. In 1991, the act was amended to eliminate discrimination in private and federal workplaces on the basis of sex, race, religion, and national origin.

civil rights movement A series of events in the United States during the fifties and sixties that brought about the Civil Rights Act of 1964.

commissioner of baseball The chief executive of baseball in charge of overseeing rules and regulations.

designated hitter A position established in 1973, the designated hitter is a player who bats in the lineup in place of the pitcher. The designated hitter rule is only used in the American League.

double A hit that results in the batter safely reaching second base.

dugout Place where the players sit during the baseball game.

error Fielding mistake made during a game by a player or team.

exhibition game Unofficial game played under regular game conditions between professional teams, usually as a part of preseason training or as a fund-raising event.

farm team A team in a system designed to train young players for the major leagues. Every major league team has a farm-club arrangement.

Gold Glove Award An award given each season to the offensive player who has made the most outstanding plays in each league.

minor leagues The farm system of major league teams where players are developed and brought up through the ranks. There are different levels, or classes, of teams.

minstrel show Popular stage entertainment in the United States in the early and mid-nineteenth century that featured comic dialogue, song, and dance, performed by a troupe of actors, traditionally composed of two white men and a chorus in blackface.

National League The older of the two major professional U.S. baseball leagues; it was established in 1876.

Reconstruction The period between 1865 and 1877 in the United States following the Civil War. The defeated South had to be rebuilt and the position of the emancipated slaves had to be defined.

runs batted in (RBIs) The number of players a batter brings around the bases to score.

segregation The practice of separating public and private spaces based on the race of the people using those spaces.

slider A fast pitch that curves slightly and sharply in front of a batter, away from the side from which it was thrown.

softball A type of baseball game played with a larger ball on a smaller field.

spring training The baseball team's program of exercise, practice, and exhibition games that takes place in the late winter and early spring, before the start of the regular season.

starting lineup The order in which each player goes to bat during the game. As the game progresses, the team's manager can replace players in the lineup.

Supreme Court The highest court in the United States; it is overseen by one chief justice and eight justices who are appointed by the president of the United States.

triple A hit that results in the batter safely reaching third base.

Voting Rights Act An act passed by Congress in 1965, making it easier for southern blacks to vote.

World Series An annual series of seven games between the winning teams of the two major baseball leagues; the first team to win four games becomes champion of major league baseball.

For More Information

The Atlanta Braves
Turner Field
755 Hank Aaron Drive
Atlanta, GA 30312
(404) 522-7630
Web site: http://www.atlantabraves.com

The Hank Aaron Chasing the Dream
    Foundation, Inc.
 Turner Field
  755 Hank Aaron Drive
 Atlanta GA 30312
(404) 522-7630

The Milwaukee Brewers
One Brewers Way
Milwaukee, WI 53214
(800) 933-7890
Web site: http://www.brewers.mlb.com

National Baseball Hall of Fame and Museum
25 Main Street
P.O. Box 590
Cooperstown, NY 13326
(607) 547 7200
(888) HALL-OF-FAME (425-5633)
Web site: http://www.baseballhalloffame.org

Web Sites

Due to the changing nature of Internet links, the Rosen Publishing Group, Inc., has developed an online list of Web sites related to the subject of this book. This site is updated regularly. Please use this link to access the list:

http://www.rosenlinks.com/bbhf/haar/

For Further Reading

Aaron, Hank. *Home Run, My Life in Pictures*. Berkeley, CA: Total Sports Ltd., 1999.

Golenbock, Peter. *Hank Aaron, Brave in Every Way*. New York: Harcourt/ Gulliver, 2001.

Rennert, Richard. *Baseball Great: Henry Aaron*. New York: Chelsea House Publishers, 1993.

Ribowsky, Mark. *A Complete History of the Negro Leagues*. New York: Birch Lane Press Book /Carol Publishing Group, 1995.

Tolan, Sandy. *Me and Hank: A Boy and His Hero Twenty-Five Years Later*. New York: Free Press/Simon & Schuster, 2000.

The Sporting News. *Baseball's Greatest Players*. St. Louis, MO: Sporting News Publishing, 1998.

Bibliography

Aaron, Hank. *I Had a Hammer: The Hank Aaron Story*. New York: Harper Paperbacks, 1991.

Ashe, Arthur Jr. *A Hard Road to Glory: The African-American Athlete in Baseball*. New York: Amistad Press, Inc., 1988.

Jones, Chipper. *Hank Aaron: A Brave Legend in the Making*. Dallas, TX: Beckett Publications, 2000.

Videos

Tollin, Michael, director. *Hank Aaron: Chasing the Dream*. VHS, Turner Home Video, 1995.

Index

About the Author

Originally from California, Lauren Spencer lives in New York City, where she teaches writing workshops in public schools. She also writes lifestyle and music articles for magazines.

Photo Credits

Cover by Bettmann/Corbis; pp. 4, 18, 24, 33, 35, 38, 66, 74, 78, 80, 84 © AP/Wide World Photos; p. 7 © The Topps Company; pp. 12, 26, 37, 47, 50–51, 53, 57, 63, 73, 79 © Bettmann/Corbis; p. 28 © *The Sporting News* Archives; pp. 40, 43 © National Baseball Hall of Fame and Museum, Inc.; p. 70 © Hulton/Archive/Getty Images; pp. 76–77 © Harry Harris/AP/Wide World Photos; p. 90 © Jacques M. Chenet/Corbis; p. 94 © Ron Edmonds/AP/Wide World Photos. Baseball Graphics: Corbis Royalty Free.

Editor

Jill Jarnow

Series Design and Layout

Geri Giordano